The Everyday
Wisdom of
Mary Aikenhead

Compiled by the Religious Sisters of Charity

First published 2007 by
Veritas Publications
7/8 Lower Abbey Street
Dublin 1
Ireland

Email publications@veritas.ie
Website www.veritas.ie

ISBN 978 1 84730 035 5

A catalogue record for this book is available from the British Library.

Printed in the Republic of Ireland by Betaprint Ltd, Dublin

Veritas books are printed on paper made from the wood pulp of
managed forests. For every tree felled, at least one tree is planted,
thereby renewing natural resources.

Contents

The Religious Sisters of Charity is a Congregation of women founded by Mary Aikenhead in 1815. They are dedicated to working with the poorest and most vulnerable people through various ministries in social/pastoral work, education and health care. In doing so they follow in the footsteps of Mary Aikenhead whose desire was to 'give to the poor what the rich could buy for money'. Today, they continue their ministry in California, Zambia, England, Ireland, Nigeria, Venezuela and Scotland.

Introduction

IN THE COURSE OF HER LIFETIME, Mary Aikenhead wrote many letters to friends, advisors, colleagues and to her Sisters. Many of the letters were written while she was confined to bed or to a wheelchair for thirteen years before her death in 1858. They reflect her own deep spirituality while at the same time offering advice, consolation, challenge and encouragement.

Today they continue to be a rich source of spirituality and contemplation for us. We are happy now to share them with a broader readership. The language, spelling, grammar and syntax of the original letters has been retained. We have made only very minor editorial changes where we felt this was essential.

We hope that all who read these daily 'Sayings' will find echoes of her vision, her energy, her sense of humour seeped through her suffering because her life was rooted in a steadfast commitment to Jesus Christ and to the service of the most weak and vulnerable people in society. We hope you will experience her spirit in the 'Sayings' we have chosen to share with you in this book.

Úna O'Neill RSC
25 May 2007

January

1

May our Lord grant us grace to repent sincerely and to begin the New Year fervently.

2

May it be the Divine Will to grant peace. Amen.

3

The work of God cannot fail.

4

The ways of the omnipotent are admirable,
may we ever bless and magnify his holy name!

5

May our Lord be praised for all
his mercies to us and to ours.

6

May it be that all of us have so prepared our
gifts and will have offered them with the holy
Kings in the Crib of Bethlehem as to merit an
increase of the Three great Virtues.

7

Let us adore and be grateful
for the many proofs of the
Sweet Providence of our heavenly father.

8

May our good God direct
and strengthen you in all to his greater glory.

9

Now as to the tattle of folk, good,
bad or indifferent, do not afflict
or alarm yourself, nor do not repine.

10

When we have so much to praise the Lord for,
we must not complain.

11

Each is in the hands of a loving and all powerful creator who knows our weakness and is ready to supply our wants.

12

May our Lord give us his holy blessings and the aid of his holy light and Divine Grace.

13

It ought with us to be a glorious thing to live and to labour for God, and so Amen!

14

Continue in His Holy name to do your little best, with confidence that He will not allow the truly humble of heart who are diffident in themselves, and only confident in His assistance, to err or to do what would be injurious to the public good.

15

May we all try to eradicate all weeds so as to make the soil of our poor hearts fit to give room and growth.

16

I have ever found that a well-timed silence in
the midst of a bustle prepares the way for a
well-timed word of explanation, which, from
those who say nothing but what is truthful,
will be more effectual than any altercation
when feelings are excited.

17

The clatter of tongues is painful.

18

Let what is good, and given to us from the hand of God and His Church, be prized and practised; time will prove its value.

19

Let us try that charity may abound in our hearts. Amen!

20

Time and steady perseverance in our duties
will deserve the blessing of divine Providence
and truth will triumph in the end.

21

May we try to learn to accept of what is bitter
to nature, with equal conformity as when it
pleases our heavenly father to visit us with
what we feel to be blessings.

22

May you enter deeply into the secrets of that
fervent love which redeemed you.

23

Thanks to our good God for all His blessings
and truly they are not of trifling account or
few, so we ought to be very holy and grateful
with our whole hearts. Are you so? Pray that
I may be.

24

Prayer is in very truth miraculously powerful
– we must be faithful in employing it.

25

Faith forbids us to repine at the ill will or evil reports of any one.

26

True affection is to rejoice in the happiness of our dear ones.

27

Never allow a sentiment of resentment to enter into our hearts.

28

We must have patience and confide all to our
Heavenly Father.

29

Pray, reflect and consult – and may the divine
spirit direct all to God's greater glory.

30

We should be wanting in gratitude to our good and merciful Lord if we did not entrust all our concerns with unlimited confidence.

31

We must try to imitate our divine model in all
things, with the assistance of His all-powerful
grace.

February

February

1

May we cling to the holy cross and try to be faithful followers of our Lord Jesus. Amen! Amen!

2

From him who supported his Immaculate Mother you are, I am certain, obtaining aid and such consolation as no human encouragement could impart.

3

We must confide in our Almighty Father and act as seems right. Amen!

February

4

Assist in regular opening of windows on every day at morning and evening availing yourselves of every ray of sunshine East and West regularly.

5

Let this holy Amen! be our constant mutual prayer.

6

May our hearts be ever grateful and may each try to prove her gratefulness by deeds. Amen!

7

May our dear Lord Jesus fill your hearts with
His own love. Amen!

8

We must pray for each other and keep praising
the eternal with cheerful hearts.

9

Thanks to our Heavenly Father for every aid
granted by His mercy to bear with and be
patient when tried by the weak ideas and
foolish freaks of temper of others.

10

May we be ever ready to receive all losses and crosses with a willing heart and gratitude for all that our good God sends us.

11

Our Heavenly Father knows how to teach each of us according to our own wants, so as to lead each to Perfection.

12

It is the work of God – may we not ever put an obstacle to its success by any infidelity of ours.

13

The true criterion of our sincerity and Purity of intention, is the degree of conformity with the Divine Will with which we receive difficulties and contradictions.

14

For myself, I have been trying to consider infirmity a blessing.

15

Gentle spring showers and continuous nourishing dews will duly serve to bring forth abundant harvest in due season.

16

Do exert the good sense with which God blessed you – but above all exercise unlimited confidence in Him, Who will never allow you to be tried above your strength.

17

In the name of the most Holy name of God
and with his powerful blessing let us proceed.

18

Pray that all may be to the
greater glory of God.

19

If all the rest of the world goes wrong, we should still persevere in trying to serve our God with Faith and fervour, trying to imitate him who came to be our Model.

20

High or low all our confidence must be in our
Lord's merciful providence.

21

Let us be fervent in praying that our Heavenly
Father who knows our great necessities, may
in mercy assist us – Amen.

22

Even in sudden emergencies the confidence of One being near who is Almighty, will support you.

23

May Our Lord prepare us for all that it shall please him to send us. Amen!

24

Keep humbly thanking his Divine Majesty for
all the very great blessings, which by his
wonderful and special mercy you and yours
enjoy.

25

We have every reason to try to depend on God alone.

26

God bless you and may you be helped and supported to do all his Divine Majesty requires.

27

May it be so by the divine blessing that the great and sudden change of weather will not have damped the cheering prospects of a greatly abundant harvest which we had apparently every reason to hope would be our blessing.

28

I hope we shall all faithfully try to prove our gratefulness by deeds.

29

Offer yourself and all freely to God.

March

March

1

May our heavenly father give us truly grateful hearts and by his all-powerful grace assist us to prove our love by deeds.

2

It is by perfect conformity to his most holy will, by a generosity of resolution, to go on in the spirit of faith whether with fewer or more spiritual gifts and favours, in the way begun of the divine service; it is only by those sentiments that we can really please God.

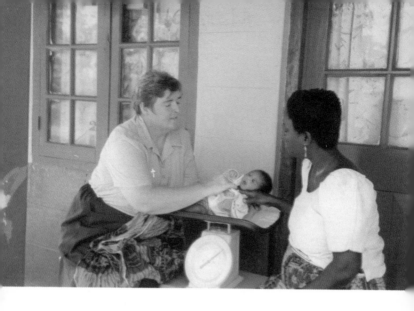

3

If we often fail, let our confidence be in Him who cannot fail and let us go on again.

4

We must confide our cares to that Almighty Providence, from whom we have always received more assistance than some of us deserve.

5

May the Lord relieve the suffering poor.

6

May our Lord teach our hearts to keep alive
the fire of grateful love and service. Amen!

7

We must ever seek council at the foot of the
cross where we are ever certain of finding an
unfailing source of Divine Grace.

8

First we must keep all sorts of weeds well cut
down in our own hearts; if any be allowed
growth therein, the seeds will shed out around
and propagate – this would be very bad.

9

Prayer is never offered without effect; offered
even by those not themselves fervent,
it is of service.

10

Our lives are just to be the Pilgrimage
through the desert.

11

We ought to be ready and willing for every
mark of the love of our Lord Jesus.

12

May we all make our journeys and changes so
as to render them so many steps towards the
right road for the Eternal Kingdom.

13

We must pray for blessings on all who assist
our efforts.

14

May Our Lord Himself help us to steer correctly through all the rock and quicksands which surround us!

15

Let us entreat of his Divine Majesty to increase our Faith – with this great gift we shall be all ready and willing to labour and to suffer, for both are necessary in carrying on the work of God.

16

We must have patience with others as He has patience with us.

17

May it be ours not to oppose the graces by which he is ready to aid us in the prosecution of his own works! Amen.

18

May our Lord teach us from all lessons sent by
His Divine Providence the true secret of entire
disengagement from all that is not of God.
Amen. Amen!

19

Bear your own temper with patience.

20

May we ever in heart and soul say Amen!

21

Let us humble ourselves and implore mercy
and forgiveness of sin.

22

God bless you and grant His holy Grace to
each around you.

23

Try to say with our Lord himself
– 'Father not my will but thine be done.'

24

Tell our Lord that it is He and He alone Who
is your support, and that your entire

confidence is in Him.

25

Let us be good, holy, humble handmaids of the ever Blessed and Immaculate Virgin Mary, and we shall sing 'Magnificat' for all eternity. Amen, Amen.

26

'Sursum Corda' even in overpowering difficulties.

27

Our prayer must be Amen to the appointments it shall please his Divine Majesty to ordain for each and all.

28

We must be imitators of the Incarnate Word from the moment in which he took on himself our human nature, until his death on Calvary.

29

May his Divine Majesty comfort you.

March

30

Better to incur the world's censure than to act
contrary to duty.

31

Under every difficulty try to Pray fervently.

April

April

1

May our Heavenly Father guide and direct all your undertakings!

2

Our crosses are all trifles in comparison to the love which redeemed us on Calvary.

3

If it be the divine will I shall rejoice at fine weather.

4

We must be patient, confiding in divine mercy
with entire conformity of heart and will.

5

May our Lord strengthen our hearts in faith
and the firm belief in the inspired word that is
his strength.

6

With the divine blessing, let us hope and confide all our cares in Him who is Almighty.

7

May our Lord give the blessings of peace.

8

May our Lord grant his own blessing and bring all to bear good fruit.

9

If we study our divine model how little account shall we be inclined to make of all that passes with time.

10

Be humble, and, as a means to become so, be as patient and as charitable as is possible.

11

Recollect that we may be fervent, though not feeling any great comfort or consolation; we have our best model in Jesus praying for support, and feeling all the weakness of poor human nature, which you and I carry about us.

12

Of little avail will be all our exertions on behalf of our suffering fellow creatures if each act does not flow from the interior spirit of genuine charity.

13

Let us try to deserve the divine blessing and then our Purity of intention and devotedness to God's most holy will, will help us to bear painful results.

14

All which is said and all the trying circumstances which arise, do not nor have not, for one second, occasioned any degree of sadness, nor led me to doubt of the care of Almighty Providence.

April

15

He Who sees all can alone judge in it,
therefore, let our cause be committed to Him
alone.

16

Never allow yourself to be overpowered by the
apprehension of an evil which may never
arrive.

17

Even if we be like stray sheep, he will take us
on his shoulders, will cure our wounds and
strengthen us to follow Him, if we have but a
sincere heart.

18

May every blessing be with and about you.

19

Self-knowledge is obtained with the help of
Divine Grace.

20

May we be ever grateful to our Lord who has
given us such solid and kindly interested
friends, so well able to advise – to themselves
also we are bound in respect and gratitude.

21

Without justice and prudence
can charity exist?

22

May his Divine Majesty be pleased to aid your
efforts to be faithful in the trial!
Amen! Amen!

23

We can praise Our Lord God for great graces
and mercies towards us individually and
generally with, I hope, sincerely grateful and
even fervent hearts in the very midst of
disappointments and contradictions.

April

24

I hope we shall say '*Fiat*' with sincere hearts.

25

We ought to keep up the Easter time in spirit and in truth for all the days.

April

26

We want great help and if we do our part He
who abides with us, can work new miracles.

27

Pray and God in his wisdom will direct you.

28

The hearts of all are in his hands whose holy providence has so wonderfully aided us all along.

29

May holy charity reign triumphant
in our poor hearts.

30

Say for me and yourself
'O Lord increase our Faith'.

May

May

1

I hope we shall all be the better of the sweet month of Mary for of course all are trying to obtain special graces for each and all and for the Poor of Christ.

2

The glory of God can be promoted by ways unknown to us and even our own sins should not lead a Christian to despair.

3

Patience is a very needful virtue and will be well learned if we try to practice conformity even in small matters.

4

May Our Lord give you all the grace to be truly grateful and humble children of his sweet Providence; may we all love this Almighty Father.

5

Our Lord who knows our need will be our help. Amen!

6

Let us try to be confident in the divine mercy, whilst we bow down in submission and to practice conformity to the divine will.

7

Pray for the gift of prudent silence and beg for the divine assistance that you may not err in words.

8

May our Heavenly Father grant His powerful
blessing to us all. Amen.

9

Why should my heart be sad, or yours either
when we know that all and every iota is
undertaken for God's honour and glory.

10

Faith and confidence will support you, and if
it be the Divine Will to exercise patience
somewhat longer, we must continue to pray
and not to faint.

11

If we act in anything worthy let us be quite content that our works may praise us not we them.

12

Pray, pray and be patient, charitable, conformed to His ever blessed will; even when tried and overpowered say twenty Amens for yourself and all of us.

13

May it be the divine will to preserve you and yours.

14

Our Lord can move even unwilling hearts and very often we see such change of feelings and even of understanding as prove the power of His Grace.

15

Oh how sincerely I praise and bless our Heavenly Father for all His care.

16

We must help each other by prayer to the ever-Blessed Virgin, our dear Mother.

17

May the great mercy and powerful aid of Divine Providence be with you and around you. Amen!

18

May our heavenly father give us truly grateful hearts and by his all-powerful grace assist us to prove our love by deeds.

19

Let us not be cast down for assuredly 'those who sow in tears shall reap in joyfulness.'

20

I hope you are assisted by the divine spirit who is I trust reigning in your heart and himself teaching you to be grateful for all he has done for you.

21

He is omnipotent and he himself has instructed us to call on him, who will help us in the hour of our need.

22

To be able to continue requires no less than Almighty and miraculous aid, may the All-Merciful Father grant that. Amen.

23

Support the weakness of each with all kindness, and try to teach all the practice of entire forbearance towards each other without which true charity will not reign.

24

He who wept for his friend will compassionate our weakness.

25

May we never act contrary to justice and truth – and may we be guided by charity in all our actions and words.

26

I hope I am properly grateful for all the share of Divine mercies which we enjoy and will duly try to be conformed to the most holy Will of our Heavenly Father in all the little or great trials which he appoints for us.

27

We must, as steadily as we can with the divine
assistance, go on in the path laid out for us.
Amen! Amen!

May

28

Our Lord is All-powerful and we must confide all our desires to his most holy will. Amen!

29

He will never cease to uphold us and to
reanimate our faith.

30

Our Heavenly Father is lovingly merciful
to us.

31

May our ever Blessed and glorious Queen and
Mother assist us to be faithful in every duty.
Amen.

June

June

1

Let us throw our embarrassments into the Sacred and loving heart of Jesus.

2

I believe our best help will be to implore without ceasing to be each hour more and more strengthened by faith.

3

We ought to pray with all our fervour.

4

You will I know unite in prayer that in all and every point, the accomplishment of what is willed by our Heavenly Father, may be our only will and prayer.

5

We ascend to the throne of love and grace in that Sacred Heart which is open to be our refuge in all our sorrows.

6

May he who holds hearts at his disposal keep ours in a state to please him.

7

Of all his lessons he desires of us to learn of
him to be meek and humble of heart.

8

Truly we have reason to be grateful. Almighty
Providence has been bountiful. May we do our
best in all ways. Amen.

9

Let us try to be very good and to pray, pray,
pray that each and all of us may do our poor
best to be faithful that is to become more and
more truly united with our God and Saviour
and devoted to His poor. Amen! Amen!

10

May we try to become more and more pleasing to the Sacred Heart of our loving redeemer.

11

May peace and resignation reign in all hearts.

12

Fear not to rely on the intellect which God has given you.

13

No one has a right to inflict great trials on others knowingly.

14

Let us thank the Almighty for all the good
spots we enjoy.

15

Divine aid is often miraculously experienced.

16

Experience proves that all our courage and strength can only come from God himself.

17

Our Heavenly Father knows our wants and our weakness but we must try to love his adorable will even under trial.

18

May we truly hunger and thirst to promote the love of his holy name in all hearts! Amen!

19

We try our best to show forth our grateful love by deeds.

20

May our Heavenly Father continue his great
mercy and care of the poor.

21

When Our Lord orders we must put out our
nets with confidence.

22

Always pray and humbly ask the Divine
assistance and a blessing will be granted to
your endeavours.

23

May our Father who is in Heaven, teach our poor weak hearts to recite the Petition 'Give us this day etc, etc' with fervour, free from all undue Solicitude and sincerely with our sole desire being to promote His own Work.

24

Meantime do the work you are about valiantly and disengage your heart from every will and wish, but, of accomplishing the holy will of God.

25

We must learn from every trade.

26

Our work would be overpowering were we to view all in any other light than as God's own work and entirely depending on the Miraculous aid of His Almighty Providence.

27

Pray the Divine Blessing on all our undertakings. Amen!

28

Our Lord will grant consolation and strength
so pray for all to God's greater glory. Amen.

June

29

I shall remind you to use the prayer of St
Peter, 'Oh Lord increase my faith.'
This divine virtue will lead us to unshaken
confidence and to perfect conformity with the
holy will of our creator.

30

Let not fear or anxiety depress you, neither allow any vain thought to find one moment's rest within your poor Heart.

July

July

1

We must confide in the Divine goodness and
do each our little best.

2

May our Lord grant a right understanding to
each and all in the moment of trial. Amen!

3

Remember that the prudence of the serpent is
to be tempered by the simplicity of the dove.

4

How my heart trembles at the awful state of our poor people and really in a sense more dreadfully do I feel about the miserable rich ones. Our duty is to pray for all and to try to get on the best we can, confiding in Almighty Providence alone.

5

Prayer from a tried heart will be very powerful.

6

We must be content and go on as fervently as we can with as much as our Lord is pleased to send.

7

Oh may we be faithful to all his divine graces.

8

Indeed the less we indulge our poor imagination on points entirely selfish, either relating to soul or body, in the same proportion we shall be happier and holier!

9

May His Holy name be ever blessed who provides all for us and may we ever love His adorable will in all He is pleased to ordain and permit.

10

We must remember not only what faith teaches, but also what hope assures us of namely an abundance of divine grace.

11

May all we undertake be for the Divine Honour and only in perfect submission to His most holy Will, for whom we live, act and labour.

12

We must not be faint hearted, we ought ever to go on with renewed Courage for the Lord will give aid in the day of our greatest weakness.

13

Pray that our Amen may be sincere.

14

We must all pray with faith and endure every iota of our anxieties and difficulties with humble patience, and above all in full charity.

15

May we all make our journeys and changes so as to render them so many steps towards the right road for the Eternal Kingdom.

16

May our Lord and his ever-Blessed Mother prosper the work.

17

We must justly be solicitous, and get all the prayers we can, then confidently lay our cares quietly before his Divine Majesty who knows what is best.

July

18

Pray and you will obtain light and wisdom
from the great source.

19

Truly we have received great graces and we are
frail vessels, but Faith, Faith. Amen.

July

20

Let us try to cherish the flame of Divine Love
in our poor hearts and we shall be
strengthened from on High, or rather we shall
feel and see all succeed under the
Mighty power of Him who Strengthens us.
Amen! Amen!

21

May our Lord direct all and strengthen you to
act in all to his greater glory.

22

Let us hourly say to him with grateful confidence, 'I can do all things in him who strengthens me.'

23

There is not nor ought there to be a resting place out of God.

24

We are not without very great blessings and supports from the Almighty Providence.

25

Pray that I may have grace to practise my preaching.

26

Oh pray that we may have a right understanding in every sense of the word.

27

I hope the true and fervent desire of practicing the most perfect conformity to the Divine Will may bring each and all to deserve great blessings from on High. Amen!

28

We must cast ourselves with confidence into his almighty care.

29

May our Good God bless you and enable you to see yourself as he sees you.

30

Commit yourself with entire confidence to His Sacred heart, desiring only to please and serve Him.

31

According to Saint Ignatius, let us all pray and labour as if all depended on our poor endeavours, and all the while, feel convinced that He alone Who is our God and the anchor of our hope, is all sufficient.

August

August

1

May our good God continue all in such peace
and joy, as will enable us to serve Him better.

2

I hope we shall each and all exceed in
generosity. Amen! Amen!

3

May we be ready to say '*fiat*'!

August

4

Thanks be to God for his great mercies! We have many to be grateful for collectively and individually.

5

Our Heavenly Father knows what is best, and may his most holy will be ours!

6

May our Lord bless and enlighten and strengthen you.

7

May our Lord provide for, guide and protect you and all of us in our various necessities.

8

We have abundant reason to keep alive our gratitude.

9

Our Great Physician is the All Powerful and All Merciful and to Him we must commit all our cares with patience and with conformity to His ever-blessed will. Our Lord will support all whose sole confidence is in him.

10

Let us pray and be very patient.

11

If I be only faithful in the space granted to me
it will suffice.

12

May you and all be vessels well prepared to receive the plenitude of the Divine Spirit –
Amen!

13

May we try to do our Lord's will purely and perfectly.

14

Well ordered charity should begin at home.

15

May our ever-blessed dear mother the Glorious Virgin Mary bestow her tender blessing on each and every one around you.

16

We pray that you may be guided to do what is best.

17

God alone must reign in our hearts and until his reign be established in them triumphantly we shall be in pain and uneasiness.

18

Painful as is the truth, we cannot act wisely, if ignorant of it.

19

I hope that the Blessed prospect of a great and good Harvest will give Heart and Courage to those who give employment. Amen!

20

May each be faithful in doing her best to keep alive peace and good will.

21

May our Lord give us all simple hearts and tongues! Amen.

22

You will not fail to obtain most precious graces for yourself and others if you have recourse to our ever-blessed Queen and dear Mother.

23

Pray and practice patience
– even towards yourself.

24

Most truly I can say that we little know when
we rise in the morning, what trials the day will
bring.

25

Do your poor best, and may the blessing of
content be with all. Amen!

26

Difficulties must be encountered in undertaking every good work but we have the Providence of an Almighty Father to depend on, and I hope your intentions will be successful.

27

May God prosper all your undertakings.

28

Those who really seek for self-knowledge cannot fail from gaining this real treasure of spiritual life.

29

In proportion as we try to turn out self and empty our poor hearts of every vain and selfish desire we shall grow in Divine love.

August

30

Let us confide in the constant care and love of
our heavenly father. Amen!

31

Your own soul, is the garden
specially given to your care.

September

September

1

Exercise unlimited confidence in him, who will never allow you to be tried above your strength.

2

Let us try by prayer to obtain a right understanding.

3

I hope in the unbounded mercy of our all powerful Lord and Father.

4

Be on your guard to keep your mind cheerful. This will improve temper and so will a moderate care of health.

5

So go on in faith and let all do their own little best.

6

Now you who have great special blessings ought to pray for those not enjoying the like.

7

We ought always try to unite ourselves with all who pray.

8

May the Glorious Queen of the Angels be your loving Mother and help you to become every day more worthy of the high dignity to which her Divine Son has called you.

9

May Our Heavenly Father give you His best
blessings and speak to your heart.

10

It would be a sort of presumption to say
'I can do all things in Him Who strengthens
me' if you were to omit the necessary exertion
on your part.

11

May we learn to speak truth when we pray.

12

May Our Lord give His Divine Blessing to our endeavours, and we must seek aid from our ever Blessed Mother.

13

Surely all about us is only transitory.

14

May we prove the power of him whose promises are to aid the weak, to support the wounded and to conquer by his holy cross.

15

May it ever be our earnest desire to learn at the foot of his cross the lessons taught to and practised by our Glorious Queen of Sorrows.

16

In all let us bear in mind that Love must be proved by deeds. Amen! Amen!

17

My poor heart is as weak as that of a chicken. Pray that I may be faithful to the end!

18

All prudence must be practised in all its shapes
by us, but we must not forget that wise
prudence requires us not to be trenchant.

19

May our Lord send you peace.

20

When our Lord is pleased to grant us the
consolation of witnessing any degrees of
success, it is our duty to be grateful,
and to bless His Holy Name
Who allows us to bear fruit. Amen!

21

I never before felt so much encouragement to cultivate the holy virtue of hope.

22

Humble yourself before God, be steady to duty; watch over your temper, and try not to allow it to influence your manner to any one.

23

May we with entire faith 'cast our care upon the Lord.'

24

May the God of peace and charity incline all hearts to keep his holy law and to do his will.

25

In the Sacred Heart of our Lord you may truly seek and find relief. Amen.

26

Let each of us be faithful in accomplishing our
respective duties towards Him,
our neighbours, and our selves;
and be ready to lay aside our active labours
when He so wills.

27

May our concerns be in the care of Almighty
Providence.

28

Let us all unite in humble petitions
for each other.

29

Pray much fervently, that our Lord may guide
and assist us in all our undertakings.

30

Let us be humble and grateful! Amen!

October

October

1

I wish we could teach folk the importance of simplicity. Truth suffers always from any deviation from beautiful simplicity.

2

We are without remedy except patience and prayer. Amen!

3

Truly we need fear no evil who are protected under the shadow of his wing, let us crouch down humbly and like the poor little chicken we may be certain of loving shelter.

4

We must rely on Almighty Providence and go on in his holy name.

5

May the Divine Mercy continue what is best
for us and incline our will to accept all His
appointments. Amen!

6

Our trust must be in the Most High.

7

May you always deserve the special protection
of our ever-glorious queen and dear mother
the Blessed Virgin Mary.

8

Try not to allow undue anxiety
to weigh you down.

9

So pray for the gift of prudent silence,
and beg for the Divine assistance
that you may not err in words.
You will require much humble patience.

10

May Our Heavenly Father guide you and
strengthen you.

11

We ought to ask for prayers and try to pray although we have faith that our Heavenly Father knows all our wants.

12

Do pray that justice may be accomplished in peace and that truth may prevail.

13

May our Lord be himself your light and your support.

14

He tells us expressly to learn of Him to be meek and humble of heart – so we need be at no loss about the virtues He loves best.

15

We must try our best to be faithful.

16

Pray, pray and get prayers – oh may we all be humbled and try to be faithful to Divine grace! Amen!

17

May our Amen be proved by deeds.

18

Time runs quickly, may we try to keep our poor lamps that is our hearts filled with the precious oil of humility and charity that we may willingly attend the first summons of the bridegroom.

19

May our Lord be our confidence.

20

May we try to be worthy and grateful partakers of the wonders which our Heavenly Father creates.

21

May we ever bless his holy name and be grateful.

22

Only that we must confide in the Miraculous
Providence of our Almighty Father I own to
you I must just faint away from the difficulties
around us.

23

Do pray and may our Lord direct
and protect us – Amen!

24

Each and all must try our best to stand steady
under the heat and burden of the day.

25

Oh may we prove our gratefulness by deeds!

26

May our Heavenly father bless and protect
you and each around you.

27

Pray for us all for many things occur almost
daily to require an exercise of many virtues.

28

May our Heavenly Father give all his blessing
and direct all to his greater glory. Amen!

29

May all spirits be truly united with him in whom we live and labour.

30

May we all be ever fervently ready to perform our little best in His service with all the generosity we are capable.

31

What we do ought to be done well.

November

November

1

What a comfort we enjoy in the communion of Saints it is an article of our precious Creed which has often raised my drooping heart.

2

To be able to save the memory of the dead which ought to be held sacred, is truly gratifying.

3

To comfort those in sorrow is merciful.

4

Let us try our best to pray and watch well. I mean by watch to do all in our power to live in the actual presence of God. Amen!

5

We must be grateful for the goods we possess.

6

The Communion of Saints is a support in the day of anxiety or affliction.

7

When by active faith you feel how near to you is our Lord, you will feel less alarmed by difficulties.

8

Our great necessity is for prayer so let us try to be good and fervent.

9

Try not to allow undue anxiety to weigh you down – exercise yourself in perfect conformity to the Divine will. Great solicitude chokes up the confidence with which we should approach to the feet of our Heavenly Father.

10

May our Lord give his divine blessing
to our endeavours.

11

Every sincere wish and prayer for health and
every best blessing to yourself
and each one around you.

12

We have need to pray and to suffer and
to labour for these are days of trial.

13

Remember we may have self esteem whilst we
speak humbly of ourselves.

14

We must try to do our best under the
confidence that our Heavenly Father will be
our strength.

15

Do your best and may our Lord guide us in all
our little doings.

16

We must try to be truly humble – not in
words but in the very core of the heart.

17

I hope that our Lord will be himself your Almighty aid.

18

Bragging and boasting and egotism ought not to be allowed to grow in our gardens.

19

May God alone influence all great and small!

20

All we can do is to try to possess ourselves in patience and with entire confidence.

21

Let us all pray with Faith and may our hope
be fulfilled. Amen.

22

May his holy name be forever praised by us
and in us. Amen!

23

Bring your mind to unremitting attention to
the Divine presence, and then when by active
faith you feel how near to you is our Lord,
you will feel less alarmed at difficulties,
you will get accustomed to call on Him for aid
to go through with each duty;
even on sudden emergencies
the confidence of One being near who is
Almighty, will support you.

24

May Our Lord teach us all to adore and love
His ever just and holy will.

25

Let us try to serve him with entire conformity,
humility and generosity.

26

To be strengthened by God we must truly live in God by actual faith and true charity.

27

The humble soul who seeks to promote the Divine honour and glory, cannot go astray.

28

Let us all unite in prayer, and may peace and resignation reign in all hearts.

November

29

Let it be our effort to creep up that narrow path in which we shall follow in the painful footsteps of Christ our King. The holy exercise will strengthen us to advance with daily increasing courage and constancy.

30

May our Lord be himself
your aid and your comfort.

December

December

1

May we learn and love the naked truth and only hate sin!

2

We have only the merciful and often truly miraculous friend and Almighty Providence to confide in, and let us pray fervently that Divine Faith may be mercifully granted to us in proportion as our confidence is exercised. Amen!

3

With His love and His Grace we truly are rich enough.

4

Our Lord can effect for us and by us more than we deserve.

5

We ought to pray that our Lord may preserve the truly abundant fruits of the earth.

6

We have all reason to be grateful and give constant praise and thanksgiving to our Heavenly Father.

7

May we ever bless and praise his Holy Name.

8

Truly we must well commit all our concerns implicitly to our ever blessed Mother and Glorious Queen. May we try our best to be faithful children of such a Mother!

9

We are the successors of eminent saints and we ought to know and emulate their virtues.

10

As to absolute perfection where can such be found – nor ought we to expect such.

11

Our duty is to be like the good Shepherd in the very parable taught us by His own Sacred Words – we must support those who are weak, and bind up the wounds and fractures of our flock, even before they complain of the pain brought on by their own folly.

12

In him who knows all we must confide.

13

We shall have the fruits of Faith, that is we
shall know how great, how holy is our God
and we shall be anxious to purify those hearts
which He has created for Himself from every
sentiment or sensation unworthy of Him.

14

May we prove our gratitude for all the favours
and mercies of the Lord.

15

We must have patience and be willing to
suffer inconvenience and delays.

16

I try to fix my confidence in the Mercy of our
loving God who is ever ready to
support His own children who try to cling
close to His Sacred Feet on Calvary.

17

Truly we need ask for no more but an increase
of Faith – all our errors arise form a want of
Faith.

18

I hope that we shall be sincerely thankful to
our Almighty Father for all the mercies of his
Divine Providence.

19

He delights to help the humble and contrite of heart.

20

May the God of peace and charity teach us to be meek and humble of heart.

21

We have a loving father, who permits the trial of poor weak nature, and is ever ready to support it when we cry out 'Lord save me I perish!' He will never cease to uphold us and to reanimate our faith.

22

Let us entreat of his Divine Majesty to increase our faith.

23

I hope that we are all united in accompanying the Blessed travellers on the road to Bethlehem and that each is faithful in trying to prepare the poor Crib in which the Infant Saviour is to take up his abode.

December

24

Oh what wonders of love and mercy shall all learn who approach to Bethlehem with simple and humble hearts.

25

Let us with the devout shepherds adore our Infant Saviour with simplicity and jubilation.

26

See how little the Infant Jesus did whilst in the Crib at Bethlehem.

27

May each and all of us try to imitate the Divine model of Bethlehem of Nazareth and of Calvary – Amen!

December

28

May every blessing be with you and yours all round you and elsewhere.

29

Thank our good God for his unfailing blessing on all our works.

30

May all our intentions and actions be directed to the greater Glory of God.

31

May we be truly grateful for all the mercies of our Heavenly Father.